The Tremulous Seasons

The Tremulous Seasons

Poetry

Terry Hauptman

P★

Polaris
Publications

www.terryhauptman.com
terry.hauptman@yahoo.com

Published by Polaris Publications,
an imprint of North Star Press of St. Cloud, Inc.

Front and back cover paintings by Terry Hauptman,
as well as interior glyphs.
Cover Design by Liz Dwyer.

ISBN 13: 9781-1-68201-100-3
ISBN 10: 1-68201-100-3

Other poetry books by Terry Hauptman

Masquerading In Clover: Fantasy of The Leafy Fool
Boston: Four Zoas. 1980
(With hand-painted plates),

Rattle
Tulsa: Cardinal Press, 1982
(With an introduction by Meridel LeSueur)

On Hearing Thunder
St. Cloud, Minnesota: North Star Press of St. Cloud, Inc., 2004
(With color plates)

The Indwelling of Dissonance
St. Cloud, Minnesota: North Star Press of St. Cloud, Inc., 2016

THE TREMULOUS SEASONS

Each story dancing a heartbeat

Each song

An opening

To love

In memory of Corinne Dwyer
and Mary McAnally.

For beloved Robert and Kira.

And for my beloved friends
Hugh and Jeanne Joudry,
Carol Heffer,
Frank Anthony,
Gerald McBride,
Barbara Clark,
Brian Fitzpatrick,
Arlene Distler,
Toni Ortner.
Mim Olsen
Claire North

Thanks to Liz Dwyer and
Curtis Weinrich for their
visionary third eyes.

The Tremulous Seasons:

AN INTRODUCTION

What name can inscribe this poet, what title inscribe her? We heard each other's plain-songs more than 30 years ago, when she sauntered Norman, Oklahoma's streets, and I sauntered Tulsa's. She heard my cries across the tornadic airwaves, and came to me. Like Emma Lazarus, she has traversed in the halls of academia and the dens of the grasslands' bandits, her statue of liberty bearing the same plaque: "give me your tired, your poor, your huddled masses yearning to breathe free." She is calling us to her, like the Great Mother.

Audre Lorde once said that if you want to know a poet, read her poetry. Come to her, dear reader, and know her in these poems. Be alert! They are spiders weaving continuity on the luminous web of life. They are Meridel LeSueur's "green corn coming into season." Like her trickster crows, she circles the world's wounds.

In Discordant, Jesus is a bird man from Santo Domingo, whose endangered thrush sings "Dide Cuedado/be more careful"). Hauptman also laments the ex-tinctures of natural life, "as sky and earth/ Embrace/ In the winds of love." She too is a bird, endangered, her discordant wings flapping in her dissonant voice.

This poetry is an act of worship, a litany of chants and psalms. Worship, like all life, incorporates a fall to the knees infused with grief and pain, anguish and remorse, anger and denial. There is also confession and absolution, as the angel of death passes over the door. These poems carry us through the circling orb of night, into the promised land of hope. Her poems remind us of "the Shoah smoke of burned hair" in the barbed wire crematoriums of Auschwitz-Birkenau ("Yom-Ha Shoah/Porajmos: Holocaust Remembrance Day"). Here one hears " a cry from the shiest angel./ A sorrow song./, the death cries heard from the gods' excuses. The reader will connect with the screeches of the caged Macaw: "I want out ! I want out!" and "Come here... human!" as the phoenix of transformation rises from the ashes of life and death.

Hauptman's voice is not first person singular. It resonates with the harmonic tremors of other writers, images of ageless visionaries, and accents of boundless named and nameless creatures. She creates here a new chat room, a new cacophony of speech for subversive linguality and life. First person plural, she keeps watch under the justice tree, guarding borders where tribes are brutally broken at night. Hear her resounding paean for peace at the shores of Mir Yam Miriam the way we pray for children under siege through the ravages of war.

The holocausts of life, strike the dark. In "Smoke," "Night/ of love and loss/ Death train/Crematorium/ Kaddish/ Yellow star/" we are devastated, as "At The Gate Of Mercy," absorbs "A rank disbelief/ In Jerusalem's narrow streets/ Longing for mists and rains/ To wash clean the blood/ Scorched in the palm of the hand."

In the world's tremulous seasons there is the lasting nuptuel of war and peace, despair and hope. Braiding traditions, Hauptman unites our separations, with her imagistic telluric tellings. This poetry is more than clarion prophecy, it resounds like Lorca's duende drumming through. Like the meditative Om... she shows us the mysterious heartbeat in us, with us. She transforms us into chicana sufis, yorubic wizards, odyssic drummers, rabbinic dancers. Navajo sherpas, taunting us to sign on for the trip.

These poems are a tuning fork, shaping a new communal song. They invite us, like a metronome ticking on our foreheads, to become practitioners of all life, all cultures, nations, eras, psyches. They guide us from the Bolivian altiplano, through the devastations of Katrina, Abu Ghraib prison to a New York hospital, from the grassroots of the Kenyon highlands, through the pine forests of Vermont, to radioactive sand dunes, an Icelandic whaling station, Fijian bridges, and the Tree of Life. She doesn't skip a beat or miss a note. She draws us like a great bow across a cosmic viola, asking us to listen.

Hauptman's musical phrasing is profound. This Lilith of the 21st century, this temptress of the hissing shriek, stalks the moors of the world, reveling and revolving, revolting and revealing. She shows us Maori rock carvings of wombs ("Heartseed") and "Rainbow Snake" lairs, whale slaughters, sacred honey ants, and Appalachian dust. This wandering Jew poet, like St. Brendan the Navigator, or Buddha, takes her place under a tree with "yellow heart-shaped leaves... with the sweetest people on earth, singing the poetry of everyday life" ("Vita Levu").

Hauptman's amen is a "so be it" not a "so long". In verse after verse she urges us into the fray, the front lines. "9/11" calls out to the East coast, "The Politics of Shame" to the Gulf Coast and the world. "Get yourself moving/through the waters/ moving/ Through troubled waters/ Get yourself moving/ journey on. . .and the cry is a howl..."

How do I wrap up this introduction? Like Hauptman does—by never ending. "With one's life one must go forward/ With one's broken life." ("Toby's Story") Hauptman has shown us here how "To bring forth the concealed heart/ of what is/Beyond the politics of lying/ The politics of dying/ Without daily language/ Into the next world" (In Coldspring Minnesota"). She has given us the map. "As the bleak light of bloodshed/ Is loosed on the world" ("Yggdrasil"), like "only the full moon," she leads us home ("Dreaming Arrivals/ Departures"). Hauptman offers her magic potions. "no milagros for loss of spirit, no limpias for spiritual cleansing," Only these poems.

—Mary McAnally, Tulsa, Oklahoma

Acknowledgements:

With gratitude to Larry Smith, editor of Caliban, for his luminous support throughout the years.

Thanks to the editors of the following publications where many of these poems first appeared:

"Altiplano," *Pemmican*, 2013.

"At Café Dante," *Caliban Online* #15; 17, 2014

"At the Cedar Lebanon Hospital," *Longhouse*, Winter, 1998.

"Blood-Star of Winter," *Vermont Views: Monkey's Cloak*, 2012.

"Buffalo Fire," "Buffalo Winds," "Ice Buffalo," "Buffalo In Warm Summer Ambers," "Windwalking: White Buffalo Calf Woman," *The Buffalo of Delaware County*, New Paintings by Frank Anthony, Poetry by Terry Hauptman, Viviana Hanson Gallery, 2010.

"By Heart," *Vermont Views Magazine: Monkey's Cloak*, Nov. 2011.

"Chimeras of False Promises and Grief," *Caliban Online* #35, April, 2019.

"Exquisite Corpse," *The Spoon River Poetry Review*, Fall 1998 "Riverwind"

"Gate of the Sun," *Caliban Online* #35, April, 2019.

"Impoverished Incantations: From The Raw Edge of Chutzpah", *Caliban Online* 14, 15, 2014.

"In Cold Spring, Minnesota," *Caliban*, Jan. 2013.

"Love Is So Powerful," *Tenth Anniversary Write Action Anthology*, 2010.

"Mirror Of Fate," *Art and Adventures Newsletter, and Advertisement for Three Artists In The Andes, The Ghosts of Licancabur, Gregory William Frux, Maria Henle, Janet Morgan*. Posted also at the Maria Henle Gallery, St Croix. Spring, 2011.

"Macaw," *Pemmican* #9, 2000.

"Mountains and Chasms: In Tune With Nature," *Vermont Views Magazine: Monkey's Cloak*, 2011.

"Onyx," *Vermont Views Magazine: Monkey's Cloak*, 2012.

"Red Stone Dancer," *Vermont Views Magazine: Monkey's Cloak*, 2011.

"Sankofa of the Mineral World," *Pemmican*, 2013.

"Shlugen Kapores," *Caliban Online* #5, Spring, 2012.

Shooting Gallery," *Pemmican* # 8, 1999 .

"Smoke," *Blackbird* 2, 2000.

"Sulphur Sky," *Caliban Online* #10, Jan. 2013.

"Toby's Story" *Blackbird* 2, 2000

"Under The Green Canopy Of Forests," *Tenth Anniversary Write Action Anthology*, 2010.

"Witness, The Ruins of Memory: Arguing With G-d," *Blackbird* 2, 2000

"Yom-Ha-Shoah/Porajmos: Holocaust Remembrance Day." *Pemmican*, 2013.

Poems

Wanderings 53

The Hunger Winter 79

xx

"The wisdom of the salamander,
Lies In your heart.
The wisdom of the toad,
Lies in your soul."

-Kira Hauptman

UNDER THE GREEN CANOPY OF FORESTS

For Wangari Maathi*

"Forests can live without us,
but we can't live without them."
-Wangari Maathi

Under the green canopy of forests
    Listening to birds fall from trees
        The salt blood of compassion
            Seeding your dreams
The blue-purple sugarcane of ancestral rains
    The mugume fig trees of Nairobi
        Call your name
The mitendu, milkev, mihugu trees
    Of Karura Forest
        Bend to women on sacred ground

"Why plant trees
    For food and firewood?"
        A force to bring down the dictatorship.*
            The grassroots of Kenya's central highlands
                Heating up.

"I found myself a woman fighting for equality.
I started planting trees
and found myself in the forefront
of fighting for the restoration of democracy
in my country."

Did the spirit winds
Bless your palms
As you praised the day?
Wangari
We are calling you

Singer of life and dreams
The roots of trees
Stare up at the sky*
We are calling you

2

The Green Belt Movement
Medicine of tribes
We are calling you
Calling you.

* Winner of the 2004 Nobel Peace Prize, Wangari Maathi (1940-2011), was a feminist human rights activist and environmentalist residing in Nairobi, Kenya. She established the Green Belt Movement which helps restore indigenous forests while helping rural women get paid to plant trees in their perspective villages. The Green Belt Movement has planted more than 40 thousand trees.

*Kenya's 24 year dictatorship

*From the Zulu

4

Deep With Inner Darkness: Quick With Inner Light

"...the special courage poetry gave me: to be wind for the kite, and kite for the wind, even when the sky is missing."

-Odysseas Elytis

6

HEART OF SKY

For Dan Carr (1951-2012)

And For Julia Ferrari

A music once heard
Continues to breathe the soul's harmonics
Molten at the edge
The lost cloud inside
The singing wind calls down angels.

Trees
Luminous as music's
Heart of sky
Breathe the deep night's resins of pines'
Flinty pitch
Crossing the river's calm
Into death's mystery
With seeds that can't grow
Until they are parched with grief

As Blue women swimming in the blood of birth
Catch river fish in their palms
Rubbed down with tinctures of the sublime
Juniper oil and gold dust
On the day of your death
Drawing you into the great mystery
Where you eternally reside.

Fire torn from the Mountain
Dreaming trees and rivers
Radiance torn as we walk softly
Into the distant thunder
Toward the dark.

How the spirit migrates
In the gnarled root of Albion's song.

Will sorrow turn to grace
As rivers burn?

AFTER YOUR DEATH

"Oh stone of the soul, our silence"
-Mahmoud Darwish

After your death
    We cared more about
        The black butterflies of compassion
            We were sensitive to the tone
                Of people's sympathy

We cared more about spider bites
        The hornet's spirit-breath
            And her paper making technique
                Listening to insects in their tequila aging cave

After your death
    We cared more about
        The owl's saxophone riff
            "Who cooks for you? Who cooks for you?"
                And the grouse's thrum,
                    In orphan winds
                        That honies the night with longing

Chewing garlic in the broken twigs of dawn
        Sitting on the stone bench of dreams
            Tasting the salt blood
                Of oil spills

Waiting for the holy rain to wash clean our fears
        Remembering what we need to remember
            Forgetting what we need to forget.

8

BLOOD-STAR OF WINTER

In Memory of Mformi Fred Yiran (1953-2011)

Who, coming out of stories hears the night
 Revealed in its breath
  That you are gone
   In the dark raven light?
    As spider's spin
     Earth and smoke
      Dear friend
       Drumming
        In the caul
         of winter.

The soul's breath
 Blanketing the wind
  You are the
   Brightest star burning
    February's sky
     Your spider eye
      Between endings
       And beginnings.

9

ONYX

For Poet Roy McBride (1944-2011)

"Love is the real power
And where there is love there
is no fear."
   -Ben Okri

August music memory's heartbeat
10   Reaching for the dark
Your last breath marking time.
You are coming back to the other world
Carrying Minnesota memory
Radiant with destiny.

Birds of the soul
Protected by night
Sing plumed owl songs of justice.

The third-eye of lunar moths lights
Love's mysteries
Deepened now by the sorrow of angels.

You are coming back from the other world
With children wearing paper-plate masks
Behind soldiers.
Your compassionate kindness sounding
Earth and winds
Singing freedom songs,
Dip your hands in the oil and wine,
Drumming forever.

AT THE CEDAR LEBANON HOSPITAL

At the Cedar Lebanon Hospital
    your mother wondered why all the
        mothers were weeping so ecstatically
            over the births of their babies
                She was sure she was the only mother who
                wanted to die.

At The Dry Harbor Nursing Home
    your mother wondered why everyone wanted to die
        She was sure she was the only one who wanted to
        live.

DREAM LIGHTNING

For Wifredo Lam (1902-1982)*

"The warm earth guards their last secrets"
—Vicente Huidobro

Why does the light flow through the
    eyes of the sleeping portrait?
The somnambulist's azure
    undulating like chance or fate
    mooncurve in the why of love

Sleeping   dancing
    Madonna of the holy image
        Dowsed gouache of the maternal language
            "la langue maternalle"
            Ecstatic immersion in the vitality
            of the universe.

Why does the light fly through
    the girl-child's salt-glaze?
        Where promise whirls
        Like so many other things unseen in this world.

Wifredo Lam was born in Sagua La Grande, Cuba, in 1902. He received his art training in Havana, Madrid, and Paris. His paintings evoke totemic landscapes, conjuring humans, animals and plants in indigenous transformations.His paintings evoke the legendary. Surrealist landscapes create a backdrop for their Indian descendents to climb up. The Jungle is a third-world version of Guernica.

12

SANKOFA OF THE MINERAL WORLD

For El Anatsui

Adrinka* aluminum bottle caps
And copper wire,
Eyedazzling wildfire:
Mountain bees
Symbols of the soul

Sankofa* of the mineral world
Casting your net across the ocean
Back to your past   13
Returning to your source
Turpentine and glaze
Gesso and tar
Attar of roses
Wasps and smoke

Ghosts unearthed at bedtime
Bird of passage
On the footpaths of red and gold
Patterned Ghanain textile
Bleeding into ancestral pots
Of near and far

As the burnt winds of caterpillar tents
Seed songs that open stars.

*Adrinka: visual symbols, originally created by the Akan of Ghana and the Gyaman of Cote
d'Ivoire in West Africa.

*Sankofa: to go back and retrieve.

LOVE IS SO POWERFUL, IT'S LIKE UNSEEN FLOWERS UNDER YOUR FEET AS YOU WALK

For Bessie Head (1937-1986)

"Love is so powerful,
It's like unseen flowers
Under your feet as you walk"
    -Bessie Head

"If I cry, who will have compassion
on me as my suffering is the suffering of others?"
    -Bessie Head

During the rainy season
    Your love for Botswana helped you look into yourself
        For goodness.
            Like Margaret, your protagonist,*
            A Massarwe in Dilepe
                Reflecting the light of love from the watery pool
                Where your parents
                Swam to you through
                The blue mists of compassion
                Your White mother locked up
                In an asylum
                    For sleeping with a Black man.*

Xosa's and Zulu's remember you
 Drawing into the carrot-seed and sweet-grass dirt,
  Growing crops in the burr-grass near the Baralong village
   Through the winding footpaths of thorntrees
    Under purple stars
     Before your ghosts got away from you
      Turning back on yourself
       Singing
        "Hey trouble,
         I see you
          want
           To sing my Blues away?"

15

"Where is the hour of the beautiful dancing birds
  in the sun-wind?"*
    As the ancestral pulse of the village tribe
     In the comings and goings of daily life
      Bows to you
       Now that you are gone.

Heat and light
  Beneath the canopy of rain
   Butterflies ablaze with destiny
    Gather up petals from the sky
     Gather up petals in your name.

*In Bessie Head's novel, *Maru*.

*In Bessie Head's novel, *A Question Of Power*: "Your mother was insane. If you're not careful you'll get insane just like your mother. Your mother was a white woman. They had to look her up, as she was having a child by the stable boy who was native."

"I had the good fortune to be born of unknown parents. People of all races brought me up. Sometimes I think like an Asian. Sometimes like a German and sometimes like a Zulu. If I could fulfill my purpose, at a later date,I shall be the truly international being."

*Bessie Head

RED STONE DANCER

For Hugh Joudry

"Sculptural energy is the mountain."
-Gaudier-Brzeska

"The eagle can hang at rest
only in the highest winds
only at the heart"
                    -Andrew Harvey

In wild light tremor
    Thunder-root of ancient hunger
        You chisel Mountain Cackler
            Crack black agate   blood agate
                Blood memory
                    Carve Easter Island in your backyard.

Jeanne Malonta sings Changing Woman
    The Abenake rabbit trickster Mahtigwess*
        Pollinates the roses
            The bone moon rattles its ancient praise.

*Mahtigwess (pronounced Metemwis)

MOUNTAINS AND CHASMS
IN TUNE WITH NATURE

For Hugh and Jeanne Joudry

"The water which arises in the mountains is the blood
which maintains the mountains of life."
                    -Leonardo Da Vinci

"Beauty, like freedom, slides sideways."
                    -Snowboarder

Climbing the mountain at night
    With your miner's headlamp
    Jeanne as your guide
    "Spontaneous mind
        Free as a bird

                I grow with it."

The mountain returns
    You return to the mountain
        Bend inward
            Climb the bone steps to the heart of the tower
                Sing with pure creative energy
                    Greet the open world with open arms
                        Nature's dynamism
                        beyond itself

Fly in your bodies
    One with the mountain
        Climb the Fire Tower
            Summer is breezy
                Stir the stars
                    Laugh in steady time to where
                    Hikers seek shelter.

Journey the druid's sarsen circle
  Pale green limestones spark the form
    Wandering in ecstasy
      Marauding in alchemy
        Dance the sacred geometries of your souls.

Always there is possibility
  The swish of lizards struck by
    The swagger of stars
      The season spins liquid amber
        Trembling through the gorge.
          Mountain sanctuary for the spirit
            On the stone bench
              The systole/diastole of the heart.

*Site-Specific. Hugh said, "Living on top of the mountain all these years, watching forest fires from the tower, taught me to see with an all-encompassing three dimensional panoramic vision, a curved arc of light, that has enriched my world-view—manifesting intuition and sustaining my creative work gazing not just straight ahead, like some unfortunate souls, looking at life from a straight line of incite-sight."

DAY OF THE DEAD

For Joel Weishaus

In the cemetery
   Behind Shalom House
      In Albuquerque, New Mexico

Tar and salt cakes for the dead.
   Children smoke
      The breath of their internment.
      Crows thunder above
         "I ain't your step-sister
         I'm your soul sister."

Night orphans with a party
   Of their own
      Dance the living embers
      In thunder and wind.

Tell me of the fire and dust sarcomas
   Of militarized dunes

Tell me of the milagros
   Of White-Sand Alamogordo
      The blasphemy of Trinity Site.

Tell me of the Angel of Death
   In the marketplace
      The black bread of dust and rain.
         Where wind bends the cedars
      And corridos of the borders
         Spark "The Deeds and Sufferings of Light."*

Tell me of the ghostly lair
   Where sagebrush and the "A bomb" bites
      The Tularosa Basin
      In the salt of night.

*Corridos/ballads of Chicano and Mexican heroes as they clash with Anglo culture, sung to me in Albuquerque by Elena Carr.

*The poetic texts and paratexts on The Aesthetics of Nuclear Technology, written in 1992 by Joel Weishaus.

SULPHUR SKY

For Carol

In dreams
    Wandering through the Jewish Community
      Of Tangier
        In the Marketplace
          And through the Calle Sinagoga
            To the city's oldest Synagogue
            House of Prayer
    In the heart of the Medina's
      Jewish corner
        And to the cafes
          Listening to ghosts
            Speaking Haketia
              The Spanish Jewish dialect
            Of Morocco
                Through the bazaars
                  Of the living moment
  Where birds fly with promise
    Through your soul

Riding your bike
    To the oldest Temple in Tunisia
      In El Grib
        On Jerba Island
          The Women's Temple
            Where treasures were held from the desert
            Where the rabbi blessed you
              And you carried this spirit
              Away with you as song.

After 9/11 Someone drove a truck
    Through the temple
        As turbulent winds
            Surround you in Vermont
            As mourning doves
                Sit on the fence of hope
                And leaves red-bud heart-shaped
                Are set ablaze
                    In the old city of
                    Blood and praise
                    War and
                        Devastating
                        Diaspora.

LEARNING BY HEART

In Salina, Kansas, light pressing the wheatfield

You press the dark earth   Elleggua*

Open the path   the crossroads yield

To the winds of chance   irregular,

Taste the seasonal winds on your tongue

Nineteen years old with your third child coming

Open the path   scatter the winds of your song

To the underworld thrum of sentinels   humming.

I sing you of pine music lit by sun

Thunder with longing for green mountain light.

Love, love the ancient branches gone

Want to know if you've ever seen this sight

Where whirling dancers bend in winter snow

You wink and cry out "I ain't spoiled for what I don't know."

*Elleggua the divine trickster-linguist in Yoruban mythology

AT CAFE DANTE

Old women chewing garlic guard the night
Meditating on coffee grounds
Listening to clave's three-two beat
Music on the street
"I said burn the chicken,burn it."

   "Give me a scorpion bowl
   With a shot of vodka and rum
   Bitter fires for the days to come."

      Writing on fire, writing on wind,
      Music in the palm of my hand
      Salts the wasp's nest
      Of pasta and snails
      Dancing the tango in a red dress
         Dolorous,
      Where the outlaw and the law are one
      Taking the dirt pill to counter Lyme Disease.

      "Don't go listening to those flaming Casssandra's
      With long blue fingernails on Asylum Street,"
      Struck down by destiny
      Wearing their necklaces of stone tears
      Eating ember-cakes
         Dispossessed
      In the ethers' prayers.

DISCORDANT

When Jésus the bird man from Santo Domingo

    Parted the feathers of the almost extinct

      Bicknell thrush

        Returning from the beautiful beaches of the Dominican

        Republic

        To the pine breezes of Vermont

        On Maniknung   sacred mountain

        The lovely bird sang

        "Dide Cuedado"

        "Be more careful"

      As sky and earth

      Embraced

      In the winds of love

A RAIN OF BLACKBIRDS

Blackbirds listening to the dead sing
Fall from the sky.
Blood on their breasts
The whoosh of broken wings
After New Year's fireworks'
Smoked bees from the wolves' dollhouse.

Blackbirds out of breath
Crashing in midair
Fall from the sky.
The earth deep in sorrow
Cries out
From the river of fate
Falling,   falling
Into gunpowder and tar
Lightning and hail
The blue fire of forgetting.
After the dazzle of New Year's
Shot of whiskey in a dirty glass,
Red-winged blackbirds cross the picket line
With a blindfold.

In Beebee, Arkansas.

26

The Tremulous Seasons

"As with the endless songs, the Navajos
spend the whole night singing, singing to the   27
wind, to the rainbow, to the lightning, animals,
maize, singing the whole night, singing that
everything is beautiful and all things are
twofold, everything is beautiful, and everything
made to join with one another, the sky, and the earth
inundated by the rain..."

-Ernesto Cardinal

BUFFALO FIRE

For Frank Anthony

"And the treaties are broken again and again
Now that the Buffalo are gone"
-Buffy Sainte-Marie

From the great plains of Buffalo fire
Nostrils flared in the memory of tribes,
Hooves kicked up in the dust of defiance.
Sparse grass in the field of loss
Mud turtles and sacred Buffalo dung.
At the center of the earth
The contour of thighs thundering
   In the power and magic
     Of the third eye.
Dark heat of bison cries
   Great wisdom of the creator
    Praising the night sky.

Walton, New York

BUFFALO WINDS

For Frank Anthony

Buffalo ride the winds
Singed in the bluesilver flames of dawn.
Look back into the torque of dreams
    Powerfully free
        On the horizon of dust.

Remembering Lakota cries
    Anishinabe and Cree
        Footfalls of your Seminole grandma
        With her bone bracelets,
           Pigeon blood, chicken skin.

           The old woman with her deer mouth
           The old woman in the ruins
           The old woman in stargrass raking the night.

           Then I saw the owl woman
           Alive in the underbrush
           Rise like moonfire running towards me.

ICE BUFFALO

For Frank Anthony

Ice buffalo know
The great wisdoms of winter
Feel it in their bones
Each hair aflame with cobalt frost.

Burnt-sienna horns pierce the dark/light
    Of winter pines
Hooves curving the deep   snow-encrusted terrain
    Of wind and salt
    Of fire and earth

Forehead pulsing with the
    Blue fire faith
    Of true believers
    Heart tricked
        By the devastations
        Of modern times.

30

BUFFALO IN WARM SUMMER AMBERS

For Frank Anthony

Buffalo in warm summer ambers
   Migrate from prehistory
Churingas, circular stones,
   Record their amblings.
Herds deep on the tamarisk plains
   Dance the fires of dawn.
Sepia, burnt-umber, sweet gum
    Resins of paint
      Brush oil and turpentine fur
        Bleed into the pitch   now blur.

WINDWALKING: WHITE BUFFALO CALF WOMAN*

For Frank "Painted Hand" Anthony

The birth of Miracle the shy baby calf
  At Rock River
    Prophecies Light Love
    Vitality
      For Native Tribes.

Lakota Sioux bless her Seventh Generation return
  As White Buffalo Calf Woman
    Ensures food, shelter and clothing.

32

As bison dream
  Their long journey of survival
    In the burning fields
      The thickets of prayer
        As The Buffalo of Delaware County
        Exude their earth-sublime
        Medicine into story.

*Miracle was born in Janesville Wisconsin, August 30, 1994. The last white buffalo calf was born in 1933; this being a heifer and all white.

The Buffalo of Delaware County, Walton, New York.

ALTIPLANO

For L.

When you were an Aymara child
  Growing up in La Paz,
    After your vapor bath
      With the quetzal singing to you
       In gentle rain,
  The priest sealed your chakras,
    Smoking out memory
        Dipping your head in the waters of fear
         Opening obediance
       To another spirit
      Another belief
        Far from your center.

Your blue tattoo of the Bolivian Zaponista's
  Burned into your arm with needles
    Your long hair cut off
      As you were taken to Isla del Sol
       In an airplane
        And handed a machete for the jungle
       Your shaman Uncle telling you
         "You will travel to the big city
          As time is circular
  Sometimes"

GATE OF THE SUN

Che Guevara
    Shapes the Bolivian altiplano,
      The quetzal flame of the centuries'
        Gate of the Sun,

"We must make ourselves into killing machines"*
    Sparking Aymara guerillas to take action.
      Then from the Isle of Pines
        Taking sanctuary before throwing
          yourself to Tupac Katari* in La Paz
            Dying each day for your peasant revolt
            And betrayed by your friends
              In the black winds of insurrection

34

Just as Luis was born in Bolivia
    Weaving his luminous
      visions
        Of the miner's lava and the condor
         Still a mystery as his twin brother
          dies coming into this world
            On a dream horse in the land of
              Simón Bolivar
                dies coming into
                  history.

*Che Guevara said these words while trying to spark his peasant revolt.

*Tupac Katari, the 18th century revolutionary, Aymaran symbol of freedom was flayed in the plaza fighting for social equality in Bolivia for the indigenous people. His last words in Aymara, were purported to be "nax jiwaiwa akat qhiparax waranq waranqanakax kutiniexa." "Now I die. In the future thousands of thousands will come after me."

MIRROR OF FATE

For the painters Greg Frux, Janet Morgan, and Maria Henle

Black Jaguar
    Dances the living embers
        Of the salt-desert's Altiplano
           Opening the dark

Chewing coca leaves
    This solar eclipse
        Under the cordillera's
           Sulfur and iron-oxide sky

Tunupha
    The Aymara God of Storms
        Strikes the wind-walking hive
           At friendship's gate
              Near the end of the world.

           God's eye
              Divining the bruja's light,
                Ancient earth
                    Painted like a prayer.

TECUMSEH'S PROPHECY

For Susan Grimaldi

The Shawnee chief Tecumseh
 Wanting to unite with neighboring tribes prophecied
  "We must unite, or the Mississippi will run backwards."
   When the Mississippi started flowing backwards
    As he proclaimed
 The tribes got together with enhusiasm and passion
  Pulsing Tsa-La-Gi
   Oklahoma's Trail of Tears.
    Choctaw, Cherokee, Chickasaw, Muskogee/Creek
   Curved towards the river
    Chasing tornadoes.

Let it be like the rain
 Let it be like the lilac night
  Restoring language
   Where it tragically was bled out.

Your Choctaw grandmother
 In the Wheelok Boarding School
  Near Tahlequah
   Wrenched from her roots
    Stripped of her spirit
   Now your drum
    Shamanically calls her to you.

*(1768-1813)

THE MASSACRE OF THE DREAMERS*

Montezuma killed the dream and the dreamers
  In the Mayan highland
    Mestizos died for seeing with their souls
      The Zinacantec's spirit-winds worth more than gold*
        Massacred that moment
          Telling their story
            Living their lives
              Dying into the
                Blood red shimmer
                  Of the sapota tree
                    Under the   37
                    Jaquar sky.

.

*In 1524 the first Spaniards arrived in what is now Guatemala

*The Mayans believe the last words Jesus said were in Mayan "eki-Lamah-Sabactani" These words were immediately translated into Spanish: "me escondo tras el pieroma de tu ser." "I'm hiding in the back of your heighest spirit."

*The Zinacantec Indians are Mayan merchants. Before the Spanish conquered them, they were involved in commerce, and made amber.

WILD FLAME TREES

"Learn, my heart, what any tree can tell you."
  -Alejandra Pizarnik

"We cast all weapons of war
We bury them from sight forever
And we plant again the tree...
Thus shall the great peace be established."
  -Iroquois

She loved weeping trees

Willows that sipped rivers

From the roots of song

The tasselled winds of Catalpas

Heavenly banyans

Desert oaks

Blood-wood eucalyptus

Ancient ginkgos

Russian olives

Ghost-gums

She loved glass apples that tasted of night

Resins of blood

From the pines and sugar maples

The fragrance of spruce and hemlock

Pierced by pine

Casharena trees   Acacia trees

The slash palm and the saw palmetto

Desert poplars

She loved the soul of trees

Wild flame trees

The language of weeping

The fires of lamentation

From the trees of life

More fire   more love

As the night drew her down

Into the great

mysteries.

EXQUISITE CORPSE

For David

"Ojalá que ser recuerdera de cosas
más grande que yo."
    -David Carney

Playing chicken tic-tac-toe on Mott Street
  You learned to speak in
    The language of birds and storms
      The secret music of chance
        Speaking Monteiro and Gaiego
          In Trás-os-Montes
            Over the mountains
              In a field of ash
                With your goat-horned memory
                  For things that never happened,
                Continuous incandescence
              Lightning and winds
                  Calling to the disappeared.

And later in Moxahala Ohio
  The wind blowing Appalachian dust
    You smell the hot road to the sagebrush
      Red earth passed Colfax, New Mexico
      On the way to Raton's ghost -breath
      And in Creola Ohio
        Appaloosa's under the wizened winds
          Dog-wood veiled like wandering brides

    Charcoal brickets
      Petrified on a coach
        Left to rot by strangers
          On their way to a funeral

I tell you "Chance is a Mask for Fate"
  As you sing me the owl's song from the eyes of G-d
    The Moorish influence singeing my soul
      Oh to be a rememberer of things more than myself

IN DIAMOND OHIO

"With heart clenched like an opened leaf."
-David

The day after the buds burst open in their splendor
And rested upon the cool breeze
The pungent surging of their leafy veins
The dog-wood veils of longing
Trying to figure out Scriabin's
Mystical 7 and augmented 4 chords
I followed a man wearing
"A Menorah Movers of America" jacket
Humming Joe Henderson's "Recuerdeme"

Through that hoop of dissonant wind
Wearing the Music of Fate
Licking the dust wherein
Dreams ride the ether
Whilst dogs carried a dead man's leg bone
Through silent spaces

SONGLINES

Alice Springs   Australia

Wandering in Dreamtime
 I follow my Great Grandfather Alexander
  A Romanian wagon painter and
   Portrait artist Jew
    Here to Alice Springs
     Ritual journey on the ancestral paths
      Passed the ghost gum trees
       The "jew-lizards"
        Fire Dreaming
         Snake Dreaming
          Eggs of the Rainbow Snake lair

The Honey-ant sacred
 That throws me back on myself from afar
  Wandering Jew
   Walking desertsongs
    With seeds of stars.

TLACHACHUCA

Without warning

As a whirlwind

Swoops on an oak

Love shakes my heart

    Sappho Fragment

Quetzal in tasselled winds ablaze   43

    In Tlachachuca

      Love shakes my heart

Without warning

    This black silk starry night

As a whirwind

    Pine-pitch blur of deer dancing

      Pico de Orizaba

        Siren pulse of longing

Swoops on an oak

    Mercedes Sosa singing

      "We're still dreaming   we're still singing

        We're still hoping"

Voladores at the Ruin s of El Tajin

Ride neon horses galloping to flames

You enter the

Blue flamed tree where

Love shakes my heart

Rub carmine into the wound

Rub indigo into the wind

This close to the star-lit music of fear

Without warning.

*The Totonac Indians named the pyramid El Tajin because of the frequency in which sun-beams fell upon the pyramid

SHATTERED MUSIC

"And gash gold-vermillion..."
'Gerard Manley Hopkins

The man wading in the river
Plays his violin
Until the sun comes down
Wading with AIDS in the river
With his peacock feather
And red roses sparking life.
Blessing dissonance
On his path of surrender
Exiled in the moment's
Earth and sky incandescence
As jackalope's drink
From the springs of witness
And night trickles down
Homeless
Into the beggar's tin cup
Raging against tomorrow
In the dying of the light.

BY HEART

For Bob and Frederic

"Why climb a mountain?
Look a mountain there:
I don't climb mountain.
Mountain's climb me
Mountain is myself
There is no mountain
nor myself.
Something moves up and down
in the air."
        -Nanao Sakaki

Climb with concentration

You who love mountains

Let them teach and embrace

Your secret selves

From their sacred centers

Sweet gum   liquid amber

Blue motion

Deep love

As the spirit passes through

PROPHETS AND SIBYLS:

THE SISTINE CHAPEL CEILING (1508-1512)

Michelangelo (1475-1564)

Candle smoke and oil

Opening up into the ceiling

Color   like shot-silk

Giving the spirit of life

Prophets and Sibyls

Single giornatas

Painted in one sitting

Speak for the Divine

Michelangelo   a devout believer

Moving backwards through time

Pushing the figures forward

To exaggerate the impact

Giving humanity a second chance

Like unborn souls in the mind of G-d

Separation of light through darkness

Of darkness through light

The soul's relationship

To the flesh

Pulled out of the shadows

By the spirit's

breath.

I said slow down some

And then slow down   some.

48

VAPORS AND AIRS:

For Leonardo Da Vinci (1452-1519)

"Shadow is of greater power than
light, in that it can impede and entirely deprive   49
bodies of light and the light can never chase
away all the shadows of bodies "*
   -Leonardo Da Vinci

Wasn't Leonardo Da Vinci a magnificent failure?
He never completed anything
He invented strange machines that couldn't run
   Because no one had a motor for them
He was an architect   painter   sculptor   inventor
   Did he worry about not pursuing one goal?
He designed parachutes before they had airplanes
   Maybe one could say, and in this way he was three centuries
   Ahead of himself,
      He jumped time.

*"A computer at the University of Amsterdam has figured out the content of the Mona Lisa's smile: 83 percent happy, 9 percent disgusted, 6 percent fearful, and 2 percent angry,"

Reported by Agence France-Presse

SACRED FURY

"Hands in the scut work."

   -Teresa Iverson

Who was Leonardo's barmaid mother?
A peasant who slept with one eye open
Drinking a shot of whiskey in a dirty glass
    "Hands in the scut work"
"You could spit in her eye and she would think its raining"
While her son painted doorways to the divine
Chewing garlic in iridescent anguish   crushing gaul wasps
      With her palm
         Bittersweet at the kitchen table
Leonardo's red chalk inward vision
    Dancing with her from Florence to Milan
Black butterflies in the sleek light
      Precipice of moans
        This never ending glimpse of mothers and sons.

50

PULSE OF WIND

For Vera Efron
(Born in St. Petersburg, Russia 1906-died in Vermont, U.S.A. 1993)

You were telling me of the winds of Black October
   How music was an iridescence
      Through the many journey's of your life
         Playing the piano with Shostakovitch
           At the St. Petersburg Conservatory
             How the pines and tamaracks
               Called you back
                 To a sacred geography of the soul.

   How you laughed climbing mountains
     In the deep calm of the moment

   How you wore the garments of the world
     With so much pride

And I knew   what it meant for me
   Walking beside you
     In beauty   eye to eye

Moondrenched
   You are gone
     And I can feel the winds turning.

52

Wanderings

"I said I'll leave. Now. With whatever:
travel sack on my shoulder; guidebook in
my pocket; camera in hand. I'll go deep
in the soil and deep in my body to find out
who I am. What I give, what I am given, and
still injustice has the greatest part.

Gold wind of life…"

-Odysseas Elytis

54

HEARTSEED:

AT RUAUMOKO'S THROAT*

near Rotorua, Aotearoa/ New Zealand

Drinking Chorus Water in New Zealand
   Listening to Kiri Te Kanawa's *
     Melodic contours of song
       The spiral pulse of music   55
We follow the river down passed the Inferno Crater
  The Waimangu   volcanic valley
     Burning with phosphorescence
       Under the pale blue to crater grey sky
    Passed the steaming lake of landslides and petrified trees
     At Nga Puia O-Te Papa
       The hotsprings of Mother earth
         Where seeds are stars
           Dreaming the heavenly waters
            The holy waters of Te Ara Mokoroa
            Maori rock carvings of wombs
Following the long abiding path of knowledge
    Into your scented room.*

*Ruaumoko is the god of earthquakes, volcanoes, and seasons in theMaori mythology of New Zealand.

*Famous Maori New Zealand Opera Singer

VITA LEVU
IN NADI, FIJI *

In Nadi, Fiji, two bridges washed out from cyclone Kina at Siga-toka and Ba. We walk passed the women's shelter at Ba, Pete's sugar field. and Singh's rice mill, drinking tea, admiring sunflow-ers under the canopy of tourists.

I take my place under the tree with the yellow heart-shaped leaves, here with the sweetest people on earth, singing the po-etry of everyday life.

But the winds take the bootleg road to where the Indian shop-keeper whose family sublet the sugar cane fields for fifty years from the Fijians, screams out "Well, what else is there to talk about... I can't get upset about all these crazy people lined up looking at themselves on the street of mirrors. Be patient, the bridges will be repaired."

Street vendors give a life-thriving "Bula" hello to each other in the whirlwind. "You got to be sly as a fox tying oneself to the un-derbelly of a cow to go through life."Who is there and not there in the splendor of becoming?" The goats near Lautoka lead the way to Suva, Salting the Soul with Fire, Dance 'till the moods of G-d pass through."

*Vita Levu, the main island in Fiji

MOUNT OLGA GORGE CENTRAL AUSTRALIA*

In the valley of the winds'
  Bloodwood and eucalyptus
    The ghost-gums' wild plumes and maili leaves
      Of the lizard ancestors
The blue-green Casuarena and Acadia trees
  Bend to the secrets of sand.

We walk the half-light laced with intuition
  Guided by voices
    Listening to the honey-ant dreaming
      Layers of sound
        As the rainbow paints the clouds
          With moving hands.

57

*The Land Rites Act of 1976 gave the Aboriginal people back the title to their country. The Olga's are 600 million years old.

HARBOR DREAM:
THE FLOATING WORLD

For Zhang Dan

Lapis blue seeds thunder
Through the veils of water
Layer upon layer
Lacquered breath
Coal black
Burning sun
In the turbulence of witness.

Bystanders watch the crushing waves of history.
The Red Guard in the foreground   with backs to us
Like in a Renaissance painting
(A repoussoir device)
Watch orphans and one-eyed crows
Scroll the swelling tide.

Thalo blue chandeliers
Tilt the luminous gaze of lovers
By the lagoon of the Emerald City.

Your murky harbor gaze
Ablaze in a mirror of smoke
The indwelling of dissonace
The ingathering of breath
Lost at the temple shrine.

Mystics and cynics conjure fireflies
In the fragrant ash of ancestral chimes.
The humors of night
Spark a child's dream with longing.
Long after The Cultural Revolution
You paint
This lightning flash
Sumi and ash
One brushstroke
Blackened by time
In a field of
poppies
And the river returns.

SONGBIRDS TRAVEL DAY AND NIGHT

Black ink shape-shifting silkworm calligraphy
   Dreams scroll the wind
      From east to west

     Through The Gate of Heavenly Peace
      Drenched in sweet decay
        Students in Tiananmen Square paint
       Winds of good-fortune

Old monks
   Bent in the willowed twilight
     Deepen in autumn

In the plum light
   Outside the city
     Spirits fly like crows

Who are these dancers spinning
   The jeweled cloud
     In the plush theatre of paradox?

In Guangzhou
   A woman wearing long earrings
     Holds the temples clay pots

Next to me on the train back to Hong Kong
   Black market cigarettes
     Scattered by birds

The student built goddess of democracy
   Blinded by her torch in both hands
     Lopes The River of Protest
       Along Chang' an Avenue

Butterflies bejeweled
   In the winds calligraphy.

*The anniversary of the student pro-democratic demonstrations of Tiananmen Square in Beijing,China,1989, was recently celebrated. The crackdown by the military that took place, killing students was witnessed recently by The Tiananmen Mothers.

HEIMAEY, ICELAND

The fish-eye spins the blinding light,
Blue lava throws the children off their stilts.
The morning orb flails earth-ash under the flow.
A thin shell of awareness covers cold in solitude,
The inner heat.
The huldufólk* who hypnotized the land
Will drink blue lightning,
Understand the dissident breach,
When diggers ply to rediscover.

*The hidden people who know that dwarves in full awareness hold up bridges.

LEVIATHAN AT THE BRINK OF MISCHIEF

"If saving the whales is called "liberal thinking"
then call me 'a liberal thinker'"
    -Bam McAnally
        ...when he was ten years old

We enter the whale cemetery
South of Akureyri.
We enter the belly of the whale,
The shadows of the wrong century.
We climb the Arctic Circle's cliff,
Death's mystery in the open sea
Bleeds before us.
Smell of whale oil ice and wind
The sky spits bone
And breaks its teeth
On the inviolate night.

      Iceland

ODIN'S RUNE

The moth seeks the light.
There is death in time:
Disillusioned realms
Light and shadow, both.

The moth slips into my eye,
Deep in the retina she spins
Darkened, inward,
Her dance of error and madness.

Death watches with two faces,
Mamifest and hidden;
Transfiguration moves freely,
Lunacy at dusk.

My eyes are wings
The mind invents.

The moth seeks the flame.
Death singes her lashes;
'Round Yggdrasil, the World Tree,
My eye fractures at the bottom of the well,
Detached.

21 Raunagata Street Rekjavik, Iceland

YGGDRASIL

World tree   Tree of life

"Steed of ygg"

Yearning for kindness and care

Gathering together

Circling the mystery of life

In this land of fire and ice

The deep roots of the heart

In Akureyre

Drinking cod-liver oil from a communal cup

In a vegetarian restaurant in Rekjavik, Iceland

Scalds circle the night with song

On Yggdrasil   The World Tree

Passed the broken bottles of winter

Thrown down next to the left

Eye of Odin

"Eg er kona sem bortha ekki kjöt."

"I am a woman who doesn't eat meat"

On 21 Ranagata in Reykjavik

"Place of Smoke"

Asta Jomsdattir serves berries and skyr

Prays for us all

As the bleak light of bloodshed

Is loosed on the world

64

DREAMING ARRIVALS/DEPARTURES

BORDERLANDS/CHOP/CHOP
MARIACI AND CUMBIA*
TINCTURES OF THE SUBLIME

Driving to Mexico City with fruit, flowers, and mesmerized chickens in the back seat of the car. I tell the chicks, "Don't worry... I'll wake you when we get to the Diego Rivera Murals at the Palace of Fine Arts. Shush, enjoy your borderland dreams, Chop/Chop, Mariachi, and Cumbia."

Following a truck carrying limes to Matamoros, the sign says, "No hay botanicas mágica." "We don't sell magic potions." Only the full moon leading us home. No "sustos pasados," milagros for loss of spirit, no limpias for spiritual cleansing, copal, incense, piñon and lime, just the tinctures of the sublime in scorched winds, fire on fire.

*Mariachi music originated in the state of Jalisco, in Western Mexico.

*Cumbia, a form of dance and music in Mexico. It has adopted versions of Colombian music like Peruvian and Argentine Cumbia.

RIO GRANDE GORGE

Wandering passed the sheep paths of yellow powder
    The sheep paths of yellow ash,
        Listening to the night heat of Indian corn
            Red-moon gazelling in the sleek light of dreams,
                I lose my way edging desert soul
                    Here, where false treaties parch memory's throat
                    Praying for rain.
Flames of the Inquisition
    Expulsion of Moors and Jews
        Spain drove out the Moors

        And expelled the Jews

        Just leave from the Port of Exile.

SKYTECH

The three-branched rod of thunder over Okemah,Oklahoma,

Home of Woody Guthrie, was a sign.

And later, as the sun went down,

The skytech struck the sky,

With her thunderous song

Where they pulled down Guthrie's house,

Brick by brick,

Because he was a communist,

In this small dustbowl town.

Years later, Arlo gets an award at "The Petroleum Club"

In Oklahoma City

His storytelling salt, a presence,

In this club where

Woody's "This Land is Your Land,

This Land Is My Land"

Would have been a joke

In this place of high rollers and elite taste

Where until recently, no Indians,

or African-Americans,

Graced the tables.

THE WHY OF OIL SPILLS

In the salt tide of tar and blood
Sand torque of turtle hunger
Plugged throat oil fate
Ash of pelican eggs parched
In carbon dust's gaul wasps
As seals struggle for oxygen
Where dolphins sniff glue
The animal heart beached
In the cemetery's unending story.

The summer sun freezes me
As water burns
And politicos pronounce
"More drilling
Deep drilling"
In the days to come.

SACRED TRASH

For Adina Hoffman

gold tooth, olive pit
broken wind
in the graveyard's craw
What's revealed/concealed
In the geniza's scar
Distilled down to ground zero.

69

9/11 GROUND ZERO
THE POLITICS OF GRIEF

When the world went dark with the towers falling
Al Queda's angerbolt   red with ash
When the world deepened with grief
When the world went dark with malevolent anguish
Falling from the depths of the day
Bodies of flames   panic and trembling   falling
In the shadow of war
In the green dark
In the shadow of disbelief
In the city of pain
Imprisoned by the news of the disappeared
In the war filled with the politics of grief
70   At ground zero   September's mourning
When the world went dark with the towers falling
        Into a mass grave
        Surge of smoke and the world forever changed
        Heartbeat and ash in the rubble decay
        The city lost in sorrow for the missing
        The city scarred on Liberty Street for the disappeared
        The city's Nassau Street carried within us.
            For these broken lives   we bear witness
            For all our world genocides
            For all our histories
            For all that we never learn from history
            For all that strikes at the heart of the common
            People
            For all our communities
            For all that strikes at the heart   the heart.

THE POLITICS OF SHAME:
WHAT SHAMELESSNESS

"If you look too deeply
Everything breaks your heart."
-Ben Okri

"We shall be given back to the old disharmony."
-Rimbaud

We shall be given back to the old disharmony
  The imprints of necessity
    As we take to the streets
      And civil rights shall be given back to the people
      Hurling life in motion
        As the circle opens before and behind
        In tragic time.

In Katrina's wake
  Hurricane forcing the levees to break
    In their fury
      The pumps fail
        The fire and transports fail
        The water and sewers fail
          As the federal government responds
          Four days late   Too late!
          FEMA* fails to come through
        For the Black and White poor
        Bending on cypress knees
          Amputees on rooftops   hanging from trees

Thousands dead inside the city of Jazz
  Créole, Mardi Grass, the Blues
    As toxic floodwaters wash bodies
      Homeless
        In Louisianna, Mississippi, Alabama,
          The Gulf Coast's home of ancestral music

From New Orleans' Superdome to Houston's Astrodome
"Wherever I am   it could be the wrong place"
  "As if the winds could turn us 'round between worlds"
  "We followed the torpor of the river

   In the devastation of winds
   Pleading as our hearts broke open."
     Wound of this world   ravaged in the politics of shame
     Evacuees desperately wait as rescue is delayed
       Air stirs   torpor and rage
        In warnings cast in dreams

  My fire lookout friends on a mountain in Vermont
   Felt the winds pick up days before
    Tasting the salt air surge   as waves swelled
     In their third eyes
       Lake Pontchartrain's bowl fills up
       And the Mississippi wails

  Get yourself moving   through the waters
   Get yourself moving   through the fear
    Get yourself moving
       Through troubled waters
        Get yourself moving
          journey on

  And the cry is for freedom
    And the cry is for love
      And the cry's in the waters
         Dark winds   firmaments

  And the cry is a howl
    And the cry is of blame
      And the cry is of witness

        In the politics of shame

*FEMA, the Federal Emergency Management Agency.

UNEARTH

"A bottomless bass chord
over the drowned ninth ward."
   -Mikhail Horowitz

"Standing in the shadows of love
waiting for the heartache to come."
   -The Four Tops

Storm-surge of Katrina's winds
   "The lower ninth ward submerged
      In a bottomless bass chord"   73
         Sludging the waters life-blood
            The pumps broke
               And Saint Charles Parish's gone
                  The old,   left drowning in their beds
                     Bound by bureaucracy's rope

Egrets on the wetlands of dissonance
   Slide the soundscape of soul
      In the dark
         Through the gates of light
            Under the black moon
               And what is the promise now?

The pink lights of Decateur are out
   As Bourbon and Esplanade
      Give way to winds

"Love, leave the re-creation of the Big-Easy
   To the people who know
      How to fix broken houses
         Fix broken hearts,
            Not Halliburton
               Do you hear?   Do you hear?"

MOANIN'
FOR THE BIG EASY: BELOVED CITY

"Two thousand enemies waiting to pull you down."
-Yoruba Oracle, Translated by Judith Gleason

Here we are in the Deep Muddy, and the
Big Fool says to press on

Protest Song during Nixon's administration

Waves break over children's playgrounds
   Undulating torrential
      Bottomless boats   drenched in decay
         Open the Big Easy
            Into a river of graves
               Into the night of winds
                  Like wolves whelping in storms

As deep music of the black keys
   Floats rafts to safety
      In the Crescent City.

Where is my beloved?
   Submerged in the lower ninth ward
      Where love drives life
         Into the tremulous dark
            "My guitar's flooded with water
            But my family's safe"

Uncompromising lightning and winds
   No compassion.
      "Fly to us Oya   goddess of life*
         Obaluaye   the dread spirit of
            Disease and earth
               Ancient goddess of nightmares and hurricanes
               Help Us!"

*Oya, the lightning queen in Yoruban spirituality who creates thunder.

74

THE BUSES ARE COMING:
THE BUSES NEVER CAME:*
REBUILDING THE CRESCENT CITY

"Where's the heart of the earth,
  I can't feel the beat
    The depth and breath of music
      Beneath my feet?"
Cried Lucia bartering for boards
        To restore her home in the French Quarter
Those submerged in the lower ninth ward
    Or in St Bernard's Parish   can't come home
And The Tremé neighborhood   the cradle of jazz
    Is gone
        But the hum and moan of survival is here
          Blanketing the night
            With falling stars

*Months later "disaster tours" run through New Orleans. Where were the buses when they were needed?

THIEVES' OIL

For Andi Anderson

With arms crossed

Thieves rubbed oil on their arms

Keeping the Bubonic Plague away
.
Tinctures of rosemary, clove,

Lemon and lavender.

76   Eucalyptus and cinnamon bark,

As Europe buried its Medieval dead

Crows pecked tar-dipped jewels,

Bees sipped grave-digger wine

In the copper and silk of time.

MACAW

We fed Houdini, the macaw, fruit loops the night his flight wing was cut off by a neighbor-woman with a red sash, its left wing broken forever, cawing in an unknown key:"Good luck pretty boy," "that music makes me nauseous," "Turn that record down, the music stinks," "I love you," "I love you," responsive as ever to human characteristics, imitating our yelps and moans as he escaped his cage,pulling out his head feathers, making himself bald, because his lover was killed in a motorcycle accident and he was in grief." To most bird lovers,Houdini was undesirable. But after cracking hazel nuts and peeling grapes, hanging out with the yellow-naped Amazon, and the cockatoo, his feathers grew back iridescent teal blue, as he, brooding, turned his back on us for not being playful enough, trickster good talkers, for lacking court and spark.

Amazon tricked the cops laughing her head off, her feathers straight up in the air, cawing "I want out! I want out!" The neighborhood cops thought there were children left alone in the trailer and busted in only to see yellow-naped Amazon brooding behind the yam-mask with her back turned towards the door. "You're not playful enough," she cawed, speaking in three voices,"Come here. . . human!" She cried out, imitating babies, teenagers, grandmothers, the gods. As Edgar Heap Of Bird's* seven dreamings fill the sky with Oklahoma music fracturing the expectation of words.

    Build
    Humble
    Center
    With
    Pulsing
    Heart*

*Hachivi Edgar Heap of Birds, a member of the Cheyenne Arapaho Nation of Oklahoma is a brilliant artist, activist, whose work confronts Racism in our culture.

The Hunger Winter

"All creative life, emotional life,
spiritual life, relational life,
moves in cycles of darkness and light,
loss and return.":

-Clarissa Pinkola Estés

PRAISE G-D FOR THE ATHEISTS
WHO RUN SOUP KITCHENS

For Geraldo

Discussing fatih-based initiatives under President Bush, my friend asked a collegue, "What about charities run by atheists? "

"What about Atheist-run soup kitchens?"

He was shocked when his colleague replied, "Why would an atheist run a soup kitchen?"

"Soup-kitchen atheists with no G-d don't exist."

"Who are these devoted optimistic unbelievers?"

This is where the narrow margins of those holding power melt away beneath the hungers of the heart, between wars, poverty. and the rigorous everyday stirring of the pots, the true gifts of faith around the kitchen table that honey the generations.

SEEDS AT ABU GHRAIB *

"Listen...
the old woman
came here
she brought seeds
in her fngernails"
    -Maurice Kenny

Before we knew about American military personnel training tor-
turers, photographing themselves abusing prisoners, Abu Ghraib
was famous as a gathering place for Iraqi farmers to commingle
their seeds, exchanging stories as they bartered for sacred-blue
grains, exchanging seeds of stars with each other. Abu Ghraib
was known as the Iraqi seed bowl perpetuating the people's fu-
ture.

Winona La Duc, spokeswoman and activist for the Anishinaabeg,
of White Earth, Minnesota, told this story of how the Unit-
ed States was replacing indigenous seeds with bio-genetically
modified strains. How important it is for us to buy wild rice from
White Earth's waters, Anishinaabeg lake-rice, not the genetically
engineered stuff. Iraqi farmers will have to buy new seeds from
Monsanto and DuPont. How the bottom line is survival. As the
mists and rains of deception loom over the world and betrayal
breeds fear and lies in the desert of desecration and war.

*The treatment of detainees at Abu Ghraib prison in Iraq, gave
legitimacy to torture until the whistleblower revealed photos of
abuses with Lynndie England holding an Iraqi prisoner, Gus, on a
leash.

---

*See Winona La Duke's work on The White Earth Recovery Project. Ban genetically mod-
ified rice, where the DNA has been taken from wild rice and domesticated trapped, stolen
into another form. Flint-corn is also endangered.

HEAT-LIGHTNING

TEACHING AT MABEL BASSETT WOMEN'S MAXIMUM SECURITY PRISON, OKLAHOMA CITY

"No hay espacio más ancho que el dolor
No hay universo como aquel que sangra

There is no space wider than that of grief
There is no universe like that which bleeds"

-Pablo Neruda

At Mabel Basset Women's Maximum Security Prison
   A vibrant woman told me:

      "I missed four hours of English as a second language
        when my husband was electrocuted."

      "I left the iron on and it burned my two year old's leg.
      My boss told me if I went home I would lose my job."

   I reached out with my young song
      The death rattle in my throat
      And all I could say was
        "Walk in Beauty."

OKLAHOMA CITY MEMORIAL:
OKLAHOMA CITY BOMBING, APRIL 19,1995 *

"We come here to remember

those who were killed, those who survived."

After feeding insects to Oklahoma armadillos
We came to the reflection pool to remember
The moment between 9:01 and 9:03 A.M.

Falling out of Time
Lost in Time

Uttering the unspeakable
As angels flew sideways
Into the arms of Passeo crows.

Burnt blossoms drive out tyrants
Marking the people's spirit
In the violet heat of charred memory
Where the world went dark with killings
Where death touches all.
Down in the bottom left corner of the soul
Where cruelty resides*
Passed the heartbeat's inner room
Where we rise up
In the blood of chilldren
In the blue corn.

*This tragedy occurred in the Alfred P. Murray Frederick Muran Federal Building on Robinson Street in Oklahoma City during working hours.

*One hundred and sixty-eight people were blown to their deaths by Timothy McVeigh who thought the United States Government had embeded computerized tracking chips in their bodies.

*"Down in the bottom left corner of the soul/Where cruelty resides." is a quote from Barbara Clark

HUNGRY MOTHER STATE PARK

"Dada todos el pan
la posada
no ahuyentéis las palomas
bayan

Give everyone bread
and lodging.
Don't scare off the doves
if they come down."

-Rosario Castellanos

Hot breath

Fullbellied

The water-drinking ghosts

Plant plastic flowers

The Great Mother breaks bread

Feeds a runaway wild birds

The Hungry Ghost trees

Battered by time

Sing Freedom Songs

Leaves veining crimson in Virginia.

UNANGEL

The night you told her

"Sleeping with you is like sleeping with a corpse"
She left her body
And began the secret writing
That marked her shame
On El Día De Los Muertos
The Day of the Dead's betrayal
Loss of faith
She became a
Martyr for Tourists
Writing Penitente Poems
With that kiss of death.

Taking the Louisville Penitentiary bus
To visit a stranger
In the serpentine silence
Of dogwood fragrance
And honeysuckle breath
"Just don't go listening to all those flaming Cassandra's"
With long blue fingernails on Asylum Street
Where the winds turned you around
In the tattooed arms of the dying dusk
Where saber-toothed crows lay their eggs
After rolling walnuts out into the traffic
To be opened by cars
While lonely sweethearts
Singing bad luck blues
Keen on firescapes
Facing G-d.

WITNESS

THE RUINS OF MEMORY: ARGUING WITH G-D

At the Jewish Cemetery in Prague

For one dollar

You buy the photo album

Of a family perished in Terezen

The child beggars that river the night

The blue light piercing

The young student Jan Palach's

Immolation in 1968

Protesting the Soviet Invasion of

Czechoslovakia.

The trains of Prague transporting Jews

In "transport" to Auschwitz

"What has become of G-d?"

"If you had known would you have cried in the face of G-d

and man that this hideousness must stop?"

*From the essay "The Children of Theresienstadt" by S. L. Wisenberg, in Witness Volume Twelve Number 1, 1998.

*Terezin (the Nazi's "model" concentration camp) 60 kilometers north of Prague, served as a transit camp for 140,000 Jews. Inmates stayed at varying lengths of times until transported to death camps. Most of those sent east from Terezin were murdered at Auschwitz.

*Jan Palach immolated himself in1968 in protest of the Soviet and Warsaw pact invasion of Czechoslavakia

*Fifty years later Family albums of Jews and Gypsies Sold for $1 at Terezin.

TOBY'S STORY

'There was earth inside them."
    -Paul Celan

"And white were those
who planned and carried out
The Holocaust genocide against the Jews, Reds,
Gypsies, and Gays in the Nazi death camps."
    -Eduardo Galeano

For Toby Weitz
...who hid under the pigs to escape Auschwitz.

We lived under the pigs
    Hidden by Polish farmers
        Under the burnt snow.
For four years we lived under the pigs
    With the slop dripping unto us
        Then finally free
           To Memory's nightmare
            "With one's life one must go forward
              With one's broken life."

SMOKE

"We Jews mustn't show our feelings,
must be brave and strong, must accept
all inconveniences and not grumble,
must do what is within our power and
trust in G-d…
Surely the time will come when we
are people again, and not just Jews."
-Anne Frank, *The Diary Of A Young Girl*

Bread and ash
Closing the eyes of the dead
In spidery winds
Jews
Wrapped in shawls
Naked to Auschwitz
Night
Of love and loss
Death train
Crematorium
Kaddish*
Yellow star

*Prayer for the dead.

AT THE GATE OF MERCY

"I walked through pomegranates,
And through your blood saw
The world burning
For love"
    -Else Lasker-Schuler

"Am I another you
And you another I?
Then let's be kind."
    -Mahmoud Darwish

90

The white flower, hatzav, opens at the Gate of Mercy

Yearning for peace

Licking pollen from the living embers

The black keys of Hesed

(Loving Kindness)

Telluric

We have lost our medicines

Rye bread and spider web pachunum*

But the winds fragrance

A rank disbelief

In Jerusalem's narrow streets

Longing for mists and rains

To wash clean the blood

Scorched in the palm of the hand.

*Yiddish for a mixture of rye bread and spider webs used for healing

ON THE STREET OF THE ETHIOPIANS:
A DOOR OPENED TO WIND

"Why is violence the only choice?
I hope by the time you read this more people
are asking this question?

I hope by the time you read this more people
are answering the question in regard to human life."
-Annice Jacoby

On the Street of the Ethiopians

   A door opened to wind

      The belly-tree of olives is a wound

        Under the canopy of night

          The blue flames of the date-palms

           Blaze as the fortunetellers amber

          Casts a shadow.

The rooster calls the day

   Pecking seeds in black earth.

     Women walk the dirt road

       In the Lebanese village of Aita al-Shaab

       In northern Lebanon

         In the twilight of war
          Surviving all this
           Knowing everything
            Could have been
             Different.

YOM-HA SHOAH/PORAJMOS :*
HOLOCAUST REMEMBRANCE DAY

"...when the revery of life
gives way to the dream of death"
    -Edmond Jabès

"Smoke, smoke higher than the feathers' of time which
the hours parade in, higher than the feathers of wind
and morning than the feathers dyed with caresses
of the dark. Smoke of incinerators, of faltering pain,
of oblivion. "Look at this smoke." said Reb. Yahid,
"the fire threw it out, and in fleeing, it maddens the fire."
    -Edmond Jabès

O the night of the weeping children!
    -Nelly Sachs

During the festival of first fruits
    The winds' shawl tasseled with greens
        Old women shrouded with fear
            Weep in the Shoah smoke
                Of burned hair
                    Remembering
                        The barbed wire   crematorium
                            Of Auschwitz Berkinau

In the tents of history

The watchers of the Dead Sea

With blue numbers on their arms

    Hear the moon break open like a love cry

The Angel at the Gate
 Bartering with Fate
  Sings Kaddish for the dead
   In The Promised Land
    While Evangelicals watching Raziel
     Bind his wrists at the Wailing Wall
      Sing the End of Days.

At the Jewish cemetery at Prague
 Where you wait at exile's gate
  Talking around the edges of pain
   The death cries born from the gods' excuses.

I heard a cry from the shiest angel
 A sorrow song

* Porajmos represents Roma remembrance of the Holocaust

HOLY WARS
NOT A LAND OF MILK AND HONEY*

"Wind at war with wind."
-Rafael Alberti

"Who is coming to kill us again?"
-Josef Hanzlik

Besieged

The olive trees drip poison and honey

Always the amnesty of music

Seeps into the zig-zag lightning of dreams.

A walk through the old walled city shatters me

Lovers perfume the dawn

And then   a roadside bomb

In the heat and light of The Promised Land

I saw their eyes glaze over

And in revenge our tribe's arsenal.

How can we sleep

As blood seeps into the earth

Drenched in disbelief

Drenched in sorrow?

*Holub e divosh, milk and honey, in Hebrew.

*Was it to be a land of fields and houses? A land of corn and wine? Of cities which they had not built and vineyards which they did not plant? Or was it to be a country of black tent and goat path? A nomad's country of milk and wild honey? A kingdom where the people may dwell in a place of their own, and move to no more?"

-11 Samuel 7:10

*Yerushalayim

SUMMER UNDER THE TREES

Licking honeysuckle at Jacques Dubois'
Children wearing goat-masks and
Horse-hair crinolines
Dance the fires of life.

Old aunties eating scallions and sour cream
Make love in blue-eyed grass.

You poke your son with a stick
Gazing at the blue number on your arm.
All these years
And still
You have learned nothing.

SHLUGEN KAPORES*

I never understood why you swung chickens
    Over your head
        Until their necks broke
            To rid yourself of sin;
                Then donated the food
                    For a neighbor's feast.

                    Why would the neighbors want these
                      Chickens
                          No prayer could cleanse?

Then I heard the hungry winds of redemption
    Trickle down
        Like blood and ash,
            Like wolves whelping in storms,
                As the sky turned red.

* Two days before Yom Kippur

IMPOVERISHED INCANTATIONS:
FROM THE RAW EDGE OF CHUTZPAH

For Max Jacob
(1876 1944)

And for Rosanna Warren

Lover of life
   Taken by the Nazi's from your monastery
     Of Saint-Benoit-sur-Loire
       To Drancy "relocation center"
        For transport

         A Catholic Jew
           Buried in your shroud of bees
            Raconteur of contradictory beliefs
            En route to the cemetery

Raking gaul wasps and smoke
   Bones and soot
     Pebbles placed on tombstones
       Eating migrant bread
         Before dying of pneumonia

Writing your impoverished incantations
   In the shadow of ruby psalms
     And one-night stands
       Situated in the center of a
        Heartbeat

Wearing your leather jacket and silk sash
   With Picasso
     On the Boulevard Voltaire
       Harlequin-trickster posed as Charlie Chaplin
        With that basilisk look of pain
         Besieged by your vision of Christ
          On Yom Kippur
           And the blood-star
            Of the Virgin's womb

As lightning struck your windowpane
    Inhaling kerosene, ether,musk and henbane
        Smoking stale tobacco with drunks, conmen,
           Alchemists, thieves,
                Friends hoping your inner-life would save you
             As you read the palms of strangers
             The Ein-Soph of the Tree of Life.

Scales fell from your eyes
    Dimmed under night skies
        Burnishing the French with Cubism
           In the vortex of history
                Genuflecting over holy water
                  Seeding the dybbuk clay
                    Never to laugh at your repentance
                      The betrayal and the turning away

As the gestapo burned books
    Robbed souls
        Crushed skulls
           In mass graves
                Gashed fate.

CHIMERAS OF FALSE PROMISES AND GRIEF

For Max Jacob (1876-1944)
And for Rosanna Warren

Chimeras of false promises and grief
  Discordant on La rue Ravignan
    Holding worms in your teeth
    As your room fills with bees,
      Cigarette smoke,incense, grease,
        Mixing paint in the urine of Baal,
          Painting portraits in the ether's cri de guerre
          With Picasso
            On the Boulevard Voltaire.

  Harlequin of Montmartre's
100 Virgin light of Sacre Coeur,
      Writing in sulfur,
        Writing in wind,
          Le cornet a dés,
          The Dice Cup
            With a stroke of a fingernail
            In the Café Le Chat Noir
            Of long-haired stars.

  Living like a poet
    At the Bateau Lavoir
      "Pray for me!"
        Your vision of Christ
          On the streets of fate.

  Dying of pneumonia
    In Drancy's internment camp
      Before transport to Auschwitz,
        Shema's yellow star
          In the mass grave's ash,
            Dreaming dirges with your somnambulist's azure,
              Your penitent gaze,
                Confessing to strange birds of prey,
                  "Hang onto my greasy feathers,
                    I know the way."

SHOOTING GALLERY

"What if nectar dripped from the corners of
grieving eyes?:"
-David Carney

The day after you grafted the tracks from your arms

Burned your hair from the inside out

Shapeshifting the black market twilight

Poised on the edge of the beginning of the end

Eating Dead Man's Bread

At the Hard Choice Cafe

Where was your soul   in what niche?

Sitting there like Chance or Fate

At the Port Authority

Take the Blue line to Chambers Street

Into that homeless cry of

Piano smoke and burned snow

Passed the sulphur fumes

In the Harmony Parking lot

Your watch set to Islamic prayer

Times.

And later with Hassids hooked on heroin

In Alphabet City at the Mo-tel   No-tell

Where your ghost jumped out of the window

"And the problem is

Every now and then

Someone would die."

"The problem with the shooting gallery is

You can't call the cops when someone dies. . .

If they raid the place

Everyone goes down.

They roll the dead out through the window

Out into the alley with the homeless,

This way no one gets arrested."

"What if nectar dripped from the

Corners of grieving eyes"

Passed the Mother's Day Special. . .

Infrared oh

"Twenty per cent off all mastectomy bras,"

Where you stand

Gesturing at nothing.

PLAYGROUND

Mother	Child, come home now Come home now or you will be grounded
First Child	In my country we are not grounded.
Mother	What country is that?
First Child	Bosnia
Second Child	In my country we are not grounded, either
Mother	What country is that?
Second Child	Vietnam
Mother	Oh, so both of you always listen to your mothers?
Third child	In my country when you are bad they cut your hair off
Mother	What country is that?

IN COLDSPRING, MINNESOTA

All those years of living on granite

With cold hearts

Your grandpa hid his Lakota Indian

Russian Jewish heritage

Here, in Coldspring, Minnesota

Passing as German to fit in.

Who would believe his stories?

Only you, his granddaughter
Know how to bring forth the concealed heart
Of what is
Beyond the politics of lying
The politics of dying
Without daily language
Into the next world.

THINKING AGAINST MYSELF AT MIDNIGHT

"What will I do with my fear

What will I do with my fear?"

-Alexandra Pizarnik

Fool of the world with your split-tongue
            spitting promise
Crying out for lost alphabets:
Thank yourself again and again   in memory and passion
So the leafy birds will sing like lava ghosts
Pushing back storms
As the seasons burn seconal.

105

Lie to yourself:
So the winds will turn you around in your sumac flame
Thinking against yourself at midnight singing
"I feel sorry for the character
Who is intimidated by a hypocrite"
Fool of the world with your split-tongue   singing.

MOONSTRUCK

I paint you the steel blue jazz-rose
Exquisitely resonant
Art and love.

I fling you the bloodrose:
That fleshy stone.

Search for me
Seek me out
I grind my blue teeth into sparks

I am the recluse tearing willow
That wild light inside the geode.

FAR CRY

Take off the tragic mask;
The dance is but hermetic tract. . .
The body still sustains the movement.
Rip off the fears,
Take off the mask.
Project the face embodied in the isolate light. . .
The screaming wind.

WINDS

"I don't know much about gods; but I think that the river…"
-T.S. Eliot

I don't know the wild winds'
    Seeds of stars
        The Talk of Gods
But I know
    When the winds take me
        Into the night
A century of fireflies
    In the hands of G-d
        Angels on salt beds
          Their eyes of fire
            Pecked by birds
              Of the besieged city
I don't know the language
    Of the dead
But I know that the river
    In the paintings of the mad
        Cries out strking the beyond.

        I don't know the way of the Gods
          But I know that the river
            In the mind of Love
              Flows back striking the within

              I don't know the ways of the Gods
                But I know that the river...

110

Terry Linda Hauptman is the author of four previous poetry collections: *Masquerading in Clover: Fantasy of the Leafy Fool*, with hand-painted plates (Boston: Four Zoas.1980), *Rattle*: (Tulsa: Cardinal Press.1982), *On Hearing Thunder* (St. Cloud, Minnesota: North Star Press of Saint Cloud, Inc., 2004), and *The Indwelling of Dissonance* (Saint Cloud, Minnesota: North Star Press of Saint Cloud, Inc., 2016).

She has a Master's degree in Poetry from The University of New Mexico, Albuquerque, and a Ph.D in Interdisciplinary Arts from Ohio University, Athens. She reads her poetry rhapsodically and exhibits her luminous Songline Scrolls nationally. She has taught World Art, Poetry, Ethnopoetics, as well as Multicultural Correspondences in Art and Poetry at several universities and workshops. She lives in Vermont with Robert and Kira Lily.

112